# BUILDING JEWISH LIFE
# Passover

by Joel Lurie Grishaver

photographs by Jane Golub, Joel Lurie Grishaver
and Alan Rowe

illustrated by Joel Lurie Grishaver

Torah Aura Productions
Los Angeles, California

*When the Holy Maggid was a Heder teacher his students really loved him. Later his students explained, "He pushed us and pulled us, asked us questions, and really listened to us—until each of us told him our own story of when we left Egypt and our own story of when we stood at Mt. Sinai."*

**For Dr. William Cutter, who taught us to tell our own stories of leaving Egypt.**

**And for David, Josh, Elana, Eitan, Judi and Alona who first gave life to these stories.**

**Thank You:**
Temple Emanuel, Beverly Hills
Rob, Mimi, Colby, Amy, Matthew and Jeremy Borden
Gabe, Lirona, and Eitan Kadosh
Esther Somlo
Kent, Grant, and Jessica Zeidman
Judi, David, and Dr. Ted Domroy
Chabad House, Westwood
Pasadena Jewish Center
Melton Research Center

**Our Advisory Committee:**
Melanie Berman, Sherry Bissel-Blumberg, Gail Dorph, Paul Flexner, Frieda Huberman, Ben Zion Kogen, Debi Mahrer, Fran Pearlman, Peninnah Schram, Joyce Seglin.

**Our contributors**
Special thanks to Alan of Alan's Custom Lab for the special printing job.

**Our Professional Services:**
copyeditor: Carolyn Moore-Mooso
Alef Type & Design
Alan's Custom Lab
Gibbons Color Lab
West Coast Graphics
Delta Lithograph

ISBN 0-933873-16-6

Library of Congress Catalog Card Number 87-040226

Torah Aura Productions
4423 Fruitland Avenue
Los Angeles, California 90058

Manufactured in the United States of America.

In each generation, every person should feel
as though he or she had actually gone out from Egypt.

*The Haggadah*

My name is Eitan and I'm 12 years old. The worst thing about being a slave in Egypt was living—I mean not living—in a house.

We lived in these little shacks made out of—it was like cardboard and mud—and every time it rained the whole thing washed away.

My name is Lirona. I'm ten. Being a slave wasn't all that bad—except that it was BORING. You had to work hard all the time—and follow every single order.

You never got to do what YOU wanted—you only got to follow orders. That is the part I hated.

My name is Gabe and I'm seven and 3/4 years old. The Hebrew word for Egypt is **Mitzrayim.** **Mitzrayim** comes from the Hebrew root—**metzar** which means a pit. **Mitzrayim** is plural.

Egypt really was the pits.

I'm Esther and I'm eight years old. When people think about slaves in Egypt—they only think about how hard it was for the men to build the Pyramids. Well we women were slaves too. My mother and I worked all day baking bread for the Egyptians—then we had to take care of our house.

When my brothers came home from a hard day on the pyramids—they didn't have to cook dinner!

My name is Judi with an i and a circle over it and I am twelve. When I was a slave in Egypt I used to dream a lot. My mother used to put me to bed at night with stories of the land that God had promised to our father Abraham.

I used to dream that those promises came true.

Kent—Age 9. When I was a slave in Egypt, I worked as a water boy in the stone quarries. I spent all day carrying a heavy jug of water from work team to work team. It was hard work—and that jar was heavy.

But I felt good about my job—because the water I carried helped to keep other Jews alive.

# PART ONE: THIS IS WHAT WE DO ON PASSOVER

This is a piece of *matzah*[1]. Matzah is the special flat bread we eat on *Pesaḥ*[2]. Pesaḥ is the Hebrew name for Passover.

When our families were slaves in Egypt and God was ready to bring us to freedom, we had to leave in a hurry. We didn't have time to knead bread and wait for it to rise. Instead, we just mixed flour and water and baked it into matzah.

*Footnotes are found on page 46.*

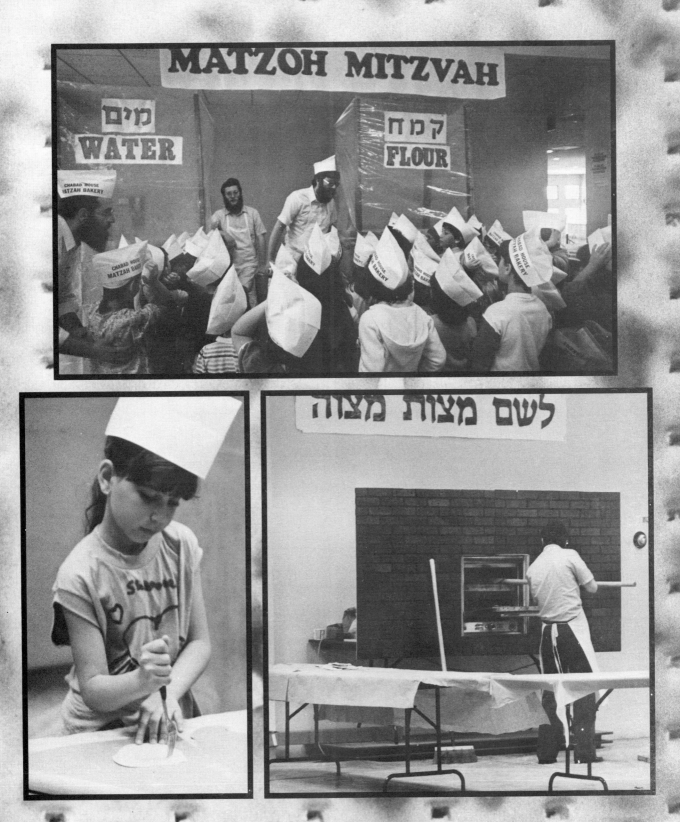

On Pesaḥ it is a *mitzvah*[3] to eat matzah. When we eat it, we remember what it was like when we were slaves in Egypt.

Because we remember the pain and suffering of slavery, we make sure that other people will not suffer in the way that we did.

Here are a feather, a wooden spoon, and a candle. We use them to get ready for Pesaḥ.

On Pesaḥ it is a mitzvah to make sure that there is no *hametz*[4] in our homes. Ḥametz is the opposite of matzah. It is stuff like bread, bagels, cookies, cakes, and crackers—things made from flour. Ḥametz is food made from dough which has had time to rise.

On the night before Pesaḥ, we search our homes for ḥametz. We make this search by candlelight. We scoop the last of the ḥametz into a wooden spoon with a feather. On the morning before Pesaḥ we burn up the last of the ḥametz.

8

This book is a *Haggadah.*[5] Haggadah means "the telling." On Pesaḥ it is a mitzvah to tell the story of how God brought all the Jewish families who were slaves in Egypt to freedom in the land of Israel. We read the story of Pesaḥ in the Haggadah.

There rose a new King over Egypt who didn't know Joseph.
He said to his people:
"Here, the nation of the families of Israel
are many and stronger than we.
Let's outsmart them,
because if there is a war they might join our enemies
and fight against us and leave this land."

*Exodus 1.8-10*

I never got to see Pharaoh—most people didn't 'cause the Egyptians thought that he was a god. And gods don't spend time visiting slaves. But I couldn't understand why he hated us. We never did anything to him. We were only a small people.

What was he afraid of? I really don't like being hated.

My job as a slave was to help make bricks. I had to go into the Nile river and scoop out mud. Then I poured the mud into molds, added straw and baked it into bricks. By the end of the day I'd have mud caked on all over my body, I'd be sweating like crazy from the heat, and there'd be flies buzzing all around me.

That was Egypt—heat, flies, and mud.

The King of Egypt spoke to the Hebrew's midwives:
"When you help a Hebrew woman deliver a baby
and you see that it is a boy, kill it. If it is a girl, it may live."

Pharaoh commanded his whole people:
"Every Hebrew son which is born you will throw in the river.
The daughters can live."

*Exodus 1.15-16, 22*

I'm proud that I'm a girl. We women were the ones who really saved the Jewish people. I worked as a secret babysitter. I took care of my baby brother and a couple of other baby boys.

The Egyptians never found any of my boys.

When I was just born, my mother hid me at the bottom of the laundry basket. When I was two, they hid seven of us boys in a cave, and my sister took care of us. When I turned three, they brought me home—but they made me wear a stupid dress. I hated that.

By the time I was five, they just let me go to work in the fields—and the hiding ended. THANK GOD.

This table is all set up for a *Seder*.[6] Seder means "order." It is the special service we have in our homes on the first night of Pesaḥ. On the table you can see candles, kiddush cups, Elijah's cup, wine, matzah, copies of the Haggadah, and the Seder plate.

At the Seder, our table becomes a place of prayer, a place of study, and a place to eat wonderful food.

Look at this Seder plate. On it you can see:
the *Z'roah*, a roasted shank bone,
the *Betzah*, an egg,
the *Maror*, the bitter herbs.
the *Ḥaroset*, a special mixture of wine, nuts, and fruit
the *Karpas*, a fresh vegtable
and *Ḥazeret*, a second kind bitter herbs.

Each of these things teaches a lesson. Each of these things help us remember another part of the Pesaḥ story.

The very first Seder took place the night before our families left Egypt. It was a scary night. No one was sure if God could really lead us to freedom.

Each family took a lamb and prepared it for dinner. They painted some of its blood on the doorposts of their house. It was a sign that this was a Jewish home. That night, the firstborn child of every Egyptian family died. So did every firstborn Egyptian animal. But, everyone living in a Jewish home was safe. So were all their animals.

*Pesaḥ* means "passed over." The name teaches us that while there was death in every Egyptian home, all Jewish homes were passed over.

On their last night in Egypt, our families ate the lamb as a **Pesaḥ offering**. They ate it along with **Matzah** and **Maror**.

# PART TWO: THE ORDER OF A SEDER

Today, when we have a Seder, there are fifteen steps.

1. קַדֵּשׁ **Kadesh:** The First Kiddush

2. וּרְחַץ **Urḥatz:** Washing Hands

3. כַּרְפַּס **Karpas:** Fresh Greens

4. יַחַץ **Yaḥatz:** Breaking the Middle Matzah

5. מַגִּיד **Maggid:** Telling the Story

6. רָחְצָה **Roḥtzah:** Washing Hands

7. מוֹצִיא **Motzi:** The Brakhah Over Bread

8. מַצָּה **Matzah:** The Brakhah Over Matzah

9. מָרוֹר **Maror:** The Brakhah Over the Bitter Herb

10. כּוֹרֵךְ **Korekh:** The Hillel Sandwich

11. שֻׁלְחָן עוֹרֵךְ **Shulḥan Orekh:** The Meal

12. צָפוּן **Tzafun:** The Afikomen

13. בָּרֵךְ **Barekh:** The Brakhot After Eating

14. הַלֵּל **Hallel:** Songs Which Thank God

15. נִרְצָה **Nirtzah:** Final Wishes

## 1. Kadesh

*Kiddush* is the brakhah over wine. Kiddush means "holy." When we say the Kiddush, we use the brakhah to remember that Pesaḥ is a holy time, a time set apart from the rest of the year.

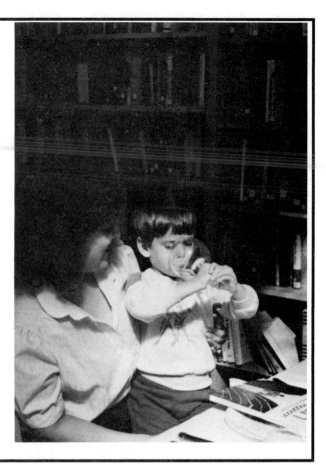

בָּרוּךְ אַתָּה יהוה
אֱלֹהֵינוּ מֶלֶךְ הָעוֹלָם
בּוֹרֵא פְּרִי הַגָּפֶן.

## 2. Urḥatz

Usually we wash our hands to get them clean. Sometimes, there are other reasons. At the Seder we wash our hands as a way of getting ready. It is a way of making the Seder a special, different, holy event. During *Urḥatz,* we say no brakhah.

*Discuss*
*What makes something holy?*
*What makes Pesaḥ holy?*
*How can blessing and drinking wine help us learn that Pesaḥ is holy?*

# 3. Karpas

At a Bar Mitzvah, a wedding, or at big formal meals, people serve a little bit of food before the real meal. They serve things like little hot dogs, dips, meatballs, herring, and gefilte fish. Usually we eat these foods with our fingers or with a toothpick. These foods are called appetizers. Their job is to *tease* our *appetites* and get us ready for the meal.

At the Seder, *Karpas* is our appetizer. We take parsley and dip it in salt water. Karpas gets us ready for the Seder by starting us thinking about the story of how we left Egypt.

Some people think that the salt water tastes like the tears that Jewish families shed when we were slaves in Egypt. Other people think that it tastes like the Reed Sea which divided when we crossed into freedom.

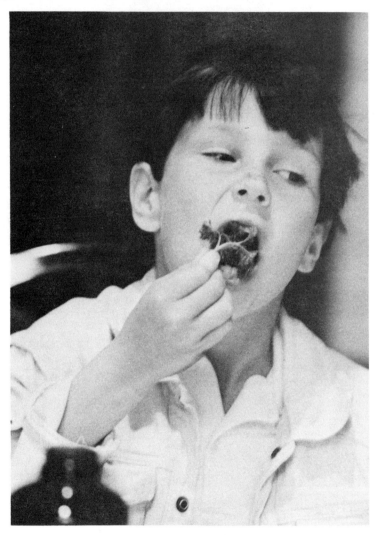

בָּרוּךְ אַתָּה יהוה אֱלֹהֵינוּ מֶלֶךְ הָעוֹלָם בּוֹרֵא פְּרִי הָאֲדָמָה.

*Discuss*
*How is Karpas like an appetizer? What does dipping parsley in salt water teach us about the Passover story?*

# 4. Yaḥatz

On the Seder table we have three pieces of matzah. During *Yaḥatz*, the leader takes the middle matzah and breaks it in half. Half of this matzah is taken away from the table and hidden. It becomes the *afikomen*, the last thing eaten at a Seder. Whoever finds the afikomen gets a prize.

During Yaḥatz, not a word is spoken.

*Discuss*
*What lesson do you think Yaḥatz teaches?*
*Why is it done?*

18

# 5. The Maggid

*Maggid* means "the telling." This is the part of the Seder where we tell the story of how God brought our families from slavery to freedom. In four different places in the Torah, we are taught that telling this story is a mitzvah. In the Haggadah, we tell this story four different ways.

The Maggid begins with these words:

> This is the bread of the poor
> which our families ate in the land of Egypt.
> All who are hungry are invited to come and eat with us.
> All who are in need are invited to come and celebrate Pesaḥ.
> Now we are here. Next year we will be in the land of Israel.
> Now we are slaves. Next year we will be free.

*Discuss*
*Why does remembering that our families were slaves and had to eat matzah cause us to invite people who are poor and people who are in need to join our Seder?*
*Read the last four sentences again. Are they talking about today or are they talking about the time of Moses?*

# The First Telling

The youngest person at the table asks four questions:

מַה נִשְׁתַּנָּה הַלַּיְלָה
הַזֶּה מִכָּל הַלֵּילוֹת.

שֶׁבְּכָל הַלֵּילוֹת אָנוּ
אוֹכְלִין חָמֵץ וּמַצָּה,
הַלַּיְלָה הַזֶּה כֻּלּוֹ מַצָּה?

שֶׁבְּכָל הַלֵּילוֹת אָנוּ
אוֹכְלִין שְׁאָר יְרָקוֹת,
הַלַּיְלָה הַזֶּה מָרוֹר?

שֶׁבְּכָל הַלֵּילוֹת אֵין אָנוּ
מַטְבִּילִין אֲפִילוּ פַּעַם
אֶחָת
הַלַּיְלָה הַזֶּה שְׁתֵּי
פְּעָמִים?

שֶׁבְּכָל הַלֵּילוֹת אָנוּ
אוֹכְלִין בֵּין יוֹשְׁבִין וּבֵין
מְסֻבִּין. הַלַּיְלָה הַזֶּה
כֻּלָּנוּ מְסֻבִּין?

Why do we make this night very different from all other nights?

On all other nights we can eat either ḥametz or matzah—
why, on this night, can we eat only matzah?

On all other nights we eat all kinds of vegetables—
why, on this night, must we eat bitter herbs?

On all other nights we do not dip vegetables even once—
why, on this night, do we dip them twice?

On all other nights we can eat either sitting up or resting on our side—
why, on this night, do we eat resting on our side?

*Discuss*
*Can you explain the last two questions? What two things do we dip at a Seder? What does it mean to eat resting on our side?*
*Can you answer all four questions?*

20

# The Second Telling

Next, the Haggadah has four different kinds of children ask four different kinds of questions. The Haggadah tells parents a different kind of answer to give each child.

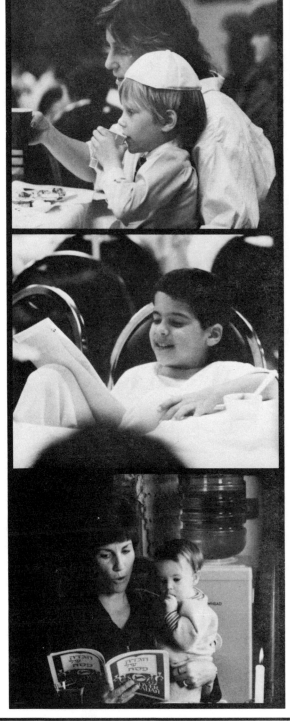

**The Wise Child:** What are the laws and rules of Pesaḥ which the Lord our God has made into mitzvot?

**Answer:** You should teach this child all the laws of Pesaḥ including the rule: "Nothing should be eaten after the afikomen."

**The Wicked Child:** What does this Seder mean **to you**?

**Answer:** Since this child says **to you** and not **to us**, the child thinks that s/he is separate from everyone else, and not part of our Jewish family. You should tell this child, "We do this because of what the Lord did for **me** when I went out of Egypt."    *Exodus 13.8*

**The Simple Child:** What is all this?

**Answer:** You should tell this child, "God took us out of Egypt, out of the land of slavery, with a mighty hand."    *Exodus 13.3*

**The child who does not know how to ask:**

**Answer:** With this child, you must begin the discussion. Tell this child, "It is because of that which the Lord did for me when I went free from Egypt."    *Exodus 13.8*

*Discuss:*
*What is wise about the first child's question?*
*What is wicked about the second child's question?*
*What is simple about the third child's question?*

*Why does the Haggadah include these four different kinds of children?*
*When have you been a wise child? a wicked child? a simple child? a child who does not know how to ask?*

Moses and Aaron went
and gathered all the elders of the Children of Israel.
Aaron repeated all the words which the Lord had spoken to Moses,
and he performed the signs in the sight of the people,
and the people trusted.
When they heard that the Lord had taken note of the Children of Israel
and that God had seen their plight,
they bowed low and gave thanks..

*Exodus 4.29-31*

The first time Moses and Aaron held a meeting on my block it was late at night. They had already put us kids to bed—but I pretended that I was asleep, then my best friend Judi and I sneaked into the meeting square and hid in an ox cart. We listened to Aaron tell what God had told Moses.

That night was the first time I ever had a dream about being free.

I once asked my parents what it meant to be a Jew—and how we got to be slaves. They took out this old sheet of parchment which was covered with names—and traced the family from Abraham, Isaac and Jacob. I know that we belong to the tribe of Benjamin. He was my great-great-great-grandfather—or something like that. Benjamin was one of Jacob's sons. Jacob became Israel after wrestling the angel—so that makes us all children of Israel.

I understand all that—but I still don't know why we're slaves.

Pharoah ordered the taskmasters,
"Do not give the people straw for making bricks anymore.
Make them go and gather straw for themselves.
Make sure they still make the same number of bricks as they have already been making."

*Exodus 5.6-8*

It was bad enough making bricks with straw. It was into the mud, out of the mud, mix the straw, pour the mud, swat the flies and then back into the mud. Without straw it was worse: It was into the mud, out of the mud, run and get the straw, mix the straw, pour the mud, and then go back into the mud.

There wasn't even time to swat the flies.

After the Egyptians made us work hard all day, I'd come home, and be almost too tired to eat supper—then I'd go to bed and cuddle my doll. Lots of nights I'd dream of the land that Moses used to tell us about.

There were streams where you could swim in milk, and a lake where you could float on honey. That would be fun.

# The Third Telling

## Next, the Haggadah has us study four verses from the Torah.

My father was a wandering Aramean,
he went down to Egypt with a few people
and lived there—
there he became a great, mighty and numerous nation.

The Egyptians were mean to us,
and made us suffer,
and gave us hard slavery.

We shouted out to the Lord,
the God of our families;
and the Lord saw our suffering,
our unhappiness,
and our oppression.

Then the Lord took us out of Egypt
with a mighty hand
with an outstretched arm
with awesome power
with signs
and with wonders.

*Deuteronomy 26.5-8*

*Discuss*
*These four sentences from the Torah only tell a small part of the story of Pesah. What other parts of this story do you know?*

# These are the ten plagues which the Holy One brought upon the Egyptians:

דָּם **Dam:** Blood

צְפַרְדֵּעַ **Tzfardey-ah:** Frogs

כִּנִּים **Ki-nim:** Lice

עָרוֹב **Arov:** Bugs

דֶּבֶר **Dever:** Cattle Disease ·

שְׁחִין **Sh'hin:** Boils

בָּרָד **Barad:** Hail

אַרְבֶּה **Ar-beh:** Locusts

חֹשֶׁךְ **Hoshekh:** Darkness

מַכַּת בְּכוֹרוֹת **Makat B'khorot:** Death of the Firstborn

**One:** Take your rod and hold out your arm over the waters of Egypt—its rivers, its canals, its ponds, all its bodies of water—that they may turn into blood; there shall be blood throughout the land of Egypt. *Exodus 7.19*

You think that all the water turning to blood might not be that bad—but can you imagine brushing your teeth with a glass full of blood? Well Dracula might like it, but the Egyptians weren't thrilled.

That's one plague down—nine to go.

**Two:** The Nile shall swarm with frogs, and they shall come up and enter your palace, your bedchamber and your bed, the houses of your courtiers and your people, and your ovens and your kneading bowls. *Exodus 7.28*

Some people think that frogs are cute. I like frogs. RIBBIT

It's hard to think of frogs as a plague—but imagine them everywhere. Imagine walking into the bathroom and finding frogs in the bathtub, frogs in the sink, frogs in the laundry basket—the Egyptians even found their toilets overflowing with frogs.

That's two plagues down—eight to go.

**Three:** Aaron held out his arm with the rod and struck the dust of the earth, and vermin came upon man and beast; all the dust of the earth turned to lice throughout the land of Egypt.

*Exodus 8.13*

Lice are really icky. I know—I've had lice. You have to wash a lot, shave off your hair, and do all this other stuff. Lice were the third plague.

Three down and seven to go.

**Four:** I will let loose swarms of insects against you and your people and your houses; but on that day I will set apart the region of Goshen, where My people dwell, so that no swarms of insects will be there.

*Exodus 8.17-18*

When plague number four came— it was the neatest thing. You could stand on the border of Goshen where it was sunny and nice and look into the rest of Egypt which was just filled with bugs. It was like we Jews had a force field.

Four down—six to go.

**Five:** All the cattle of the Egyptains died, but none of the cattle of the families of Israel died. When Pharaoh asked, he found that not a head of the cattle of the families of Israel had died; yet Pharaoh remained stubborn. He would not let the people go.

*Exodus 9.6*

This is the fifth plague; five down, five to go—

but I don't want to talk about it. Dead cattle are gross.

**Six:** Take handfuls of soot and throw it toward the sky in the sight of Pharoah. It shall become a fine dust all over the land of Egypt, and cause boils on man and beast. *Exodus 9.8-9*

Did you ever have an itch you couldn't scratch? Itches can be the worst thing—worse than a deep cut—worse than a broken bone. An itch can be real torture. When the Egyptians got boils—they all itched all over. Six down—four to go.

**Seven:** Moses held his rod toward the sky, and the Lord sent thunder and hail and fire down to the ground. The hail was very heavy with fire flashing in the middle of it. *Exodus 9.23*

Now this is what I call a good plague. Hail killed all the crops, and hurt alot when it hit you. But what I liked best was the fire that appeared in the midst of the ice. God really does colossal special effects.

I gave this plague a "10," even thought it was only plague number seven.

**Eight:** Locusts will cover the surface of the land. No one will be able to see the land. They shall eat all the crops which are left after the hail. They shall eat away all your trees that grow in the field. *Exodus 10.4-5*

You would have thought that by this point the Egyptians would have gotten smart. So far they had gone through eight plagues. They've had blood, frogs, lice, insect swarms, dead cattle, boils, hail and now locusts. But Pharaoh was dumb—he wanted more.

**Nine:** Moses held out his arm toward the sky and thick darkness fell on all the land of Egypt for three days. People could not see one another, and for three days no one could get up from where he or she was—but all the families of Israel enjoyed light in their dwellings.

*Exodus 10.22-23*

I'm supposed to tell you what the nineth plague was like. To tell the truth I don't remember.

I do remember the next day though. Moses gave us this order from God—to go to our neighbors and borrow all the silver and gold and jewels we could.

It was lots of fun—"excuse me Nefertiti, but could I please borrow a cup of gold and a dozen rubies."

It was great—they were so scared that they gave it to us, even more than we asked for.

Then God told Moses who told Aaron to order us to get ready for a Seder, and to paint the blood of the Pesaḥ lamb on our doorpost.

That night was the first time that Jews ever celebrated Passover. We were still slaves in Egypt, but we had a meal and a service, ate biter herbs and ate matzah. I asked the four questions— and got a dollar from Uncle Asher when I found the afikomen.

In the middle of the Seder we heard this screaming. Screaming from everywhere. It was so awful that I started to cry. My mother held me tight.

**Ten:** In the middle of the night the Lord struck down all the firstborn in the land of Egypt. There was no house where there was not someone dead. *Exodus 12.29-30*

## DAYYENU
How many good things God has done for us!

אִלּוּ הוֹצִיאָנוּ מִמִּצְרַיִם — דַּיֵּנוּ

**Ilu hotzi-anu mi-mitzrayim—dayyenu**
Had God only taken us out of Egypt—DAYYENU.

אִלּוּ נָתַן לָנוּ אֶת הַשַּׁבָּת — דַּיֵּנוּ

**Ilu natan lanu et ha-shabbat—dayyenu.**
Had God only given us the Shabbat—DAYYENU.

אִלּוּ נָתַן לָנוּ אֶת הַתּוֹרָה — דַּיֵּנוּ

**Ilu natan lanu et ha-Torah—dayyenu.**
Had God only given us the Torah—DAYYENU.

אִלּוּ הִכְנִיסָנוּ לְאֶרֶץ יִשְׂרָאֵל — דַּיֵּנוּ

**Ilu hi'khni-sanu l'Eretz Yisrael—dayyenu.**
Had God only brought us to the Land of Israel—DAYYENU.

*Discuss*
*Dayyenu means, "it would have been enough." In others words, this song says, that if God had only done this one thing, it would have been amazing and more than enough—but God did more. What things in your own life can you say "Dayyenu" about?*

# The Fourth Telling

Rabban Gamliel was one of the rabbis who wrote down and put together the Seder we use today. He taught:

Three things must be explained during the Seder.
These three things are **Pesaḥ**, **Matzah**, and **Maror**

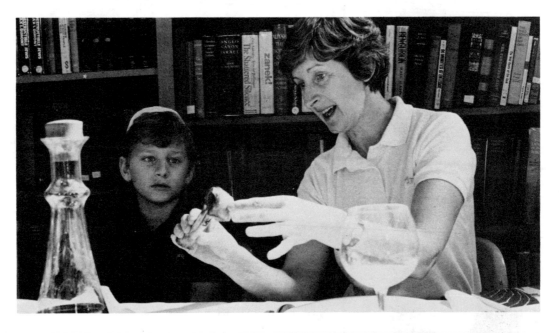

## 6. Roḥtzah

Now we are almost ready to eat. Every Jewish meal begins with bread. Since we are just about to eat the matzah, we wash our hands and get ready to eat. This time we do say a brakhah.

בָּרוּךְ אַתָּה יהוה אֱלֹהֵינוּ מֶלֶךְ
הָעוֹלָם אֲשֶׁר קִדְּשָׁנוּ בְּמִצְוֹתָיו
וְצִוָּנוּ עַל נְטִילַת יָדָיִם.

*Discuss*
*The roasted shank bone stands for the Pesaḥ-offering. What part of the Pesaḥ story does it teach?*
*What does the Matzah teach us?*
*Maror is the bitter herb. What does the Maror teach us?*

# 7. Motzi

Because we are about to eat the matzah, we say *ha-motzi*, the brakhah we say before eating any kind of bread.

בָּרוּךְ אַתָּה יהוה אֱלֹהֵינוּ מֶלֶךְ הָעוֹלָם הַמּוֹצִיא לֶחֶם מִן הָאָרֶץ.

# 8. Matzah

We have learned many lessons about matzah. We know that it was the food baked the last night in Egypt. We know that it reminds us of when we were slaves. We know that it urges us to help the poor and those in need. Just before we eat the matzah, we say one more brakhah. This brakhah reminds us that eating matzah and learning its lessons is a mitzvah.

בָּרוּךְ אַתָּה יהוה אֱלֹהֵינוּ מֶלֶךְ הָעוֹלָם אֲשֶׁר קִדְּשָׁנוּ בְּמִצְוֹתָיו וְצִוָּנוּ עַל אֲכִילַת מַצָּה.

31

## 9. Maror

In the Torah we are told, "The Egyptians made slaves of the children of Israel. They made their life bitter with hard slavery—slaving with cement and bricks and in the fields." On Pesaḥ it is a mitzvah to eat maror, the bitter herb, and remember. The brakhah reminds us that this, too, is a mitzvah.

בָּרוּךְ אַתָּה יהוה אֱלֹהֵינוּ מֶלֶךְ הָעוֹלָם אֲשֶׁר קִדְּשָׁנוּ בְּמִצְוֹתָיו וְצִוָּנוּ עַל אֲכִילַת מָרוֹר.

*Discuss*
*What lesson does haroset teach?*
*What can we learn from the "Hillel Sandwich?"*

## 10. Korekh

At the very first Seder in Egypt, our family ate the Pesaḥ-offering together with *matzah* and *maror*. In the Seder described in the Talmud, we learn that they also added *haroset*. Ḥaroset is a special mixture of nuts, fruit, and wine. It reminds us of the cement we used to glue the bricks together when we were slaves in Egypt.

Hillel was another one of the rabbis who helped to write down and put together the Seder we now follow. He used to eat matzah and maror together, just like they did at the first Seder. We do just as he did.

Many families also mix in the ḥaroset.

## 11. Shulḥan Orekh

*Shuḥan Orekh* means "the set table." This is when the famous Seder question, "When do we eat?" can be answered, "Now!"

Families serve their favorite Pesaḥ foods. This means chicken soup and matzah balls, chopped liver, turkey, brisket, tzimmes, kishke—there are many wonderful possibilities.

## 12. Tzafun

*Tzafun* means "hidden." This is where the children look for the afikomen which was hidden all the way back in the beginning of the Seder. The winner usually gets a reward.

## 13. Barekh

It is a mitzvah to say a brakhah both before and after eating. We call the brakhot said after the meal, *Birkat Ha-Mazon*. Barekh is when we say *Birkat Ha-Mazon*.

בָּרוּךְ אַתָּה יהוה אֱלֹהֵינוּ מֶלֶךְ הָעוֹלָם הַזָּן אֶת הַכֹּל.

When I left Egypt, I took my next door neighbor's ruby.

When I left Egypt, I took my next door neighbor's ruby and some matzah.

When I left Egypt, I took my next door neighbor's ruby, some matzah, and my teddy bear.

When I left Egypt, I
took my next door
neighbor's ruby,
some matzah,
my teddy bear,
and the parchment
with all the names of
my whole family.

When I left Egypt, I
took my next door
neighbor's ruby,
some matzah,
my teddy bear,
the parchment
with all the names of
my whole family,
and my memories of
being a slave.

When I left Egypt, I
took my next door
neighbor's ruby,
some matzah,
my teddy bear,
the parchment
with all the names of
my whole family,
my memories of
being a slave,
and a roll of toilet
paper.

Seriously—it was a
good idea. Who
knew how how long
we'd have to camp
out?

## 14. Hallel

The word "Halleluyah" comes from the Hebrew word *Hallel*. It means, "Praise the Lord." Hallel is a group of songs which thank God for everything which was done for us.

Just before Hallel, we open the door for Elijah, and invite him to drink from a cup which has been waiting for him. Since before the Seder began, Elijah's cup has been filled and waiting. Elijah was a prophet. Stories tell that he will come back to us and announce the beginning of a time when everyone will live in peace.

## 15. Nirtzah

שָׁלוֹם  *Shalom* is the Hebrew word for peace.

יְרוּשָׁלַיִם  *Jerusalem* is the name of the capital of Israel.

If you look very closely at the Hebrew letters which spell *Jerusalem*, you can see the word *shalom*. Jerusalem is the city of peace.

*Nirtzah* is the final step in the Seder. We drink the fourth cup of wine and sing, "*L'shanah Ha-bah Birushla-yim*," Next year in Jerusalem—Next year may we all live in the city of peace.

# PART THREE: ACTIVITIES

## PESAḤ, MATZAH, MAROR

Each of these three symbols teaches us an important lesson about being a Jew. **Match the symbol with the lesson.**

PESAḤ      פֶּסַח

Being a slave was a bitter life.

MATZAH      מַצָּה

When God took us out of Egypt, we had to leave in a hurry.

MAROR      מָרוֹר

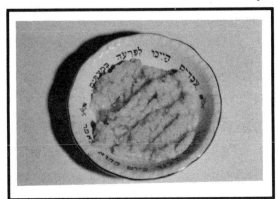

God "passed over" the houses of the families of Israel.

# Ḥaroset

Jews in different parts of the world make different kinds of ḥaroset. Here are four different recipes (thanks to Harvard Hillel Children's School)

## Ḥaroset from Eastern Europe

1/2 cup shelled walnuts
3 large apples
1/4 cup sweet red wine
cinnamon

*Chop and mush to taste.*

## Ḥaroset from Yemin

9 oz. sesame seeds
2 1/4 lbs. pitted dates
1 lb. raisins
1 cup chopped almonds
1 cup chopped walnuts
4 tsp. ground cinnamon
1/2 tsp. ground cloves
1/2 tsp. ground ginger
1/2 tsp. ground cardamon
salt to taste
water as needed

*Toast sesame seeds over medium flame, stirring frequently in pan until evenly brown.*
*Add sesame seeds to other ingredients in a large pot.*
*Add enough water so that mixture resembles preserves.*
*Cook over low flame for 15 minutes.*

## Ḥaroset from Turkey

1/2 cup pitted dates
2 cups chopped apples
1/2 cup dried appricots
1/2 cup chopped walnuts
water

*Cook fruit with just enough water to cover it until soft enough to mash. Mash with fork and blend. Add nuts.*

## Dessert Ḥaroset from Eretz Yisrael

2 chopped apples
6 mashed bananas
1 juiced and grated lemon
1 juiced and grated orange
1 1/4 cup chopped dates
4 tsp. chopped candied orange peel
nuts
1 cup red wine
matzah meal
2 tsp. cinnamon
sugar

*Blend the fruits and nuts.*
*Add wine*
*Add as much matzah meal as the mixture will take and still remain soft.*
*Add cinnamon and sugar to taste.*
*Mix well and chill before serving.*

# TWO CHANCES TO HELP OTHERS

Every Jewish holiday has its own way of reminding us to give *Tzedakah* and help others. Getting ready for Pesaḥ gives us two different ways of giving tzedakah.

If you want to celebrate Pesaḥ, you need lots of special food. You have to get rid of all your ḥametz and make sure that everything is *Pesaḥdik*, ready for Pesaḥ. This can be expensive.

*Ma'ot Ḥittim* is a special tzedakah collection taken just before Pesaḥ. It is money which helps poor Jews celebrate Pesaḥ.

Also, when we clean out all the ḥametz from our homes, we have a lot of good food which we can't use. Many Jews take their ḥametz and give it to shelters, soup kitchens, and other places which feed the hungry.

The prayer *Ha'laḥma an'ya* is found on page 19. Read it again before answering these questions.

What Pesaḥ wish do we help to make come true when we give money to ma'ot ḥittim?

What Pesaḥ wish do we help to make come true when we give our ḥametz to poor non-Jews?

*Parents should help their children answer the next two questions. If necessary, you may have to research these answers.*

One way we can help poor Jews celebrate Pesaḥ is _____

_____

One way we can use our ḥametz to help poor non-Jews is \_\_\_\_\_

_____

# THE ORDER OF SEDER

Fill in this chart.

**1.** Kadesh

We drink the first cup of wine.

**2. Urḥatz**

We wash our hands.

**3.** Karpas

We dip parsley in salt water

**4. Yaḥatz**

We break the Middle Matzah.

**5.** Maggid

We tell the story of Pesaḥ in four different ways:
Four Questions
Four Children
Four Biblical Verses
Rabbi Gamliel's Three Things + the beginning of Hallel.
We drink the second cup of wine.

**6. Roḥtzah**

We wash our hands.

**7.** Motzi

We say the brakhah for bread.

**8. Matzah**

We say the brakhah for the mitzvah of eating Matzah.

9. _maror_

   We say the brakhah for the
   mitzvah of eating bitter herbs.

10. **Korekh**

    We eat a sandwich of matzah,
    maror, and ḥaroset.

11. **Shulḥan Orekh**

    We eat the Meal.

12. _Shulhan Orekh_

    We hunt for and find the afikomen.

13. **Barekh**

    We say the brakhot after eating.
    We drink the third cup of wine.

14. **Hallel**

    We welcome Elijah.
    We sing songs which praise and
    thank God.

15. _Nirtzah_

    We drink the fourth cup of wine.
    We finish the Seder.
    We wish for next year in Jerusalem.

**Kadesh**

**Urḥatz**

**Karpas**

**Yaḥatz**

**Maggid**

**Roḥtzah**

**Motzi**

**Matzah**

**Maror**

**Korekh**

**Shulḥan Orekh**

**Tzafun**

**Barekh**

**Hallel**

**Nirtzah**

# MY EXODUS

On Pesaḥ we learn how to feel like the Jews who were slaves in Egypt. Tell your own story of what it was like to be a slave.

*Parents should help students by writing down their answers.*

## PARENT

When I was a slave in Egypt, my job was _to build pyramids._

The one thing I hated most about being a slave was _that I had to listen to other people all the time._

Even though it was horrible being a slave, the one thing which kept me going was _the thought of one day being free._

The one thing which being a slave taught me was _to appreciate freedom and choices._

## CHILD

When I was a slave in Egypt, my job was _to do whatever anyone asked me to do._

The one thing I hated most about being a slave was _I couldn't do anything I wanted._

Even though it was horrible being a slave, the one thing which kept me going was _I got to work alot_

The one thing which being a slave taught me was _never give up. Keep trying_

# BUILDING JEWISH LIFE

## A Partnership

This **Building Jewish Life** Curriculum is designed with the belief that the best possible Jewish education comes to be only when the classroom and the home are linked. These pages are designed to cycle back and forth between those two realms, and to be used as a tool for learning in each. For this material to work most effectively, teacher and parent must assume interlocking roles and share in actualizing Jewish values and expressions. Each will do it in his/her own way. Each will do it with his/her own style. Together, they will reinforce each other, offering the child tangible experience and understanding of a visionary tradition.

## Mitzvah Centered

*Mitzvot* is a word which means "commanded actions" and is used to describe a series of behaviors which Jewish tradition considers to be obligations. Classical Judaism teaches that the fabric of Jewish life is woven out of 613 of these mandated actions. This series is built around the *mitzvot*, but it uses the term somewhat differently. In our day and age, the *authority* behind any "command" or obligation is a matter of personal faith and understanding. Each Jew makes his/her own peace or compromise with the tradition, affording it a place in his/her own life. In our age, the *mitzvot* have become rich opportunities. They are the things which Jews do, the activities by which we bring to life the ethics, insights, and wisdom of our Jewish heritage. Such acts as blessing holiday candles, visiting the sick, making a seder, comforting mourners, feeding the hungry, hearing the Purim megillah, studying Torah, educating our children, and fasting on Yom Kippur are all part of the *mitzvah—Jewish-behavior—* Jewish "opportunity" list. They are actions which, when they engage us, create moments of celebration, insight, and a sense of significance. It is through the *mitzvot* that the richness of the Jewish experience makes itself available. Without addressing the "authority" behind the *mitzvot*, and without the mention of "obligation," this series will expose the power of many *mitzvah*-actions and advocate their performance based on the benefit they can bring to your family. We do so comfortably, because we know that you will explore this material and make decisions which are meaningful for you and your family.

## The Classroom

In the classroom, this volume serves as a textbook. It helps the teacher introduce major objects, practices, personalities and places in Jewish life. It serves as a resource for exploring Jewish values and engages the students in "making-meaning" from Jewish sources. The inclusion of both a parent's guide and a teacher's guide at the end of this volume was an intentional act. We felt it was important for parents to fully understand that which is being taught in the classroom.

## The Home

This material suggests three different levels of home involvement. On the simplest level, it contains a number of parent-child activities which demand your involvement. They cannot be completed without your help. None of these are information centered. The task of teaching names, pronunciations and facts has been left for the classroom. Rather, these are all moments of shar-

ing values and insights or experimenting with the application of that which has been learned in class. They should be wonderful experiences and they call upon you to be a parent interested in his/her child, not a skilled teacher or tutor.

On a second level, much of this material can also be used as "read-aloud" experiences at bedtime, or as the basis for family study and discussion at the dinner table. Do not be afraid to "pre-empt" that which will be taught in class, or to "review" that which your child has learned. The more reinforcement, the better.

Finally, and most dramatically, there is the experience of participating in the *mitzvot* described in this book. We strongly urge you to make this a year to "try-out" as many of them as possible. Think of them as the field-trips and home experiments which will enrich the classroom experience and make it comprehensible.

## The Network

The prime focus of this text is celebration. Celebrations are better when they are shared with friends. New activities and new challenges are easier when they are shared. Old activities are also enriched by the presence of others. Many of the congregations which adopt this series will already have a system of Havurot, Jewish Holiday Workshops, or family activities. Others, will organize parallel parent education sessions and special events for the families of the students in this program. We also imagine that some families will network with their friends to "try-out" some of these *mitzvah*-events. It is our *strong suggestion* that at least on an event to event basis, you connect with other Jewish families to experience some of the celebrations about which your child will be learning.

# PASSOVER

Passover is an intrusive holiday. It makes a lot of demands: telling you what to eat, what not to eat, and requiring the most extended and complicated ritual performance that is ever expected by an individual Jewish family. Passover is a demanding holiday, not only taking up a week of your life, but also requiring extensive preparation, organization and even a post-holiday cleanup period. It is a celebration which asks you to spend money and time, not allowing you to limit your involvement to just getting dressed up and showing up at the right time. Passover is obsessive; it wants to redefine your world view. Passover intrudes itself into your daily life. During Passover week you can't escape its reality. Matzah is everywhere. Matzah crumbs fill your experience. Passover practices limit and shape your actions. In the process of doing so, its message—a message of freedom, dignity, community and responsibility—embeds itself again into your priorities. When you come to think about it, it is probably worth the effort.

The Passover story itself is very simple, "We were slaves to Pharaoh in Egypt; but the Lord our God brought us forth with a mighty hand and with an outstretched arm." On Seder night, our national experience becomes part of the story of our family history. In the same way, we have sat through countless tellings and retellings of the stories of how Mommy met Daddy, of the day that Jackie was born, and of the time that Grandma brought a bunk bed home from downtown on the subway. Passover provides children with the opportunity to again ask their parents, "Tell us the story of when we were slaves in Egypt." Gathered in families, sitting in homes, we transform the national history of the Jewish people into the story of our family. The Exodus becomes "up close and personal," it becomes colored with private jokes, special recipes, original rituals, and dozens of other elements which make it ours. The Passover celebration gives us ownership of the Jewish story and its messages, for it is our story—the one that we tell to our children in our own way just as our parents told us in theirs. That is why the two-part essence of the Passover celebration is (1) for "Every person to see him/herself as if s/he personally went out from Egypt" (*Haggadah*) and (2) "You shall tell your child...it is because of what the Lord did for me went I went free out of Egypt." (*Exodus* 13.8)

## THREE OPPORTUNITIES

Maimonides, the medieval Jewish scholar who provided us with a major systematization of the 613 mitzvot, lists eight which involve the celebration of Pesah. Six of these concern the removal of hametz, one involves the eating of matzah, and one involves the telling of the story of the Exodus to our children. In addition, there are other mitzvot which are actualized on Pesah: resting on a

festival, the addition of extra worship opportunities on a festival, and the *mitzvah* of counting the *Omer*, part of the process of tithing agricultural produce. However, it is through three major activities, (1) the eating of matzah, (2) the elimination of hametz, and (3) the telling of the Exodus story, that Passover works its magic.

The Eating of Matzah: Matzah is a food with stories to tell. It is as simple as food gets; just take flour, add water, knead and bake. The recipe doesn't even say, "Salt to taste." Despite the simplicity, or because of it, it has much to teach.

Matzah is mythically rooted in the flight from Egypt, being the quick provision made by our ancestors when they had to leave at a moment's notice. (*Exodus* 12.39) Matzah was the primal Jewish fast-food. Its taste is the experience of last-minute flight. It is the flavor of the Exodus experience.

Matzah is part of the first Passover. On their last night in Egypt, in the terror of a final watch night of not knowing, Jewish families gathered in their homes and cele-

brated a first Seder. This was the night of the tenth plague, the night that death would visit every Egyptian home. It was a night of death and terror. To keep their homes safe, each family had dipped a hyssop plant in the blood of a lamb and painted its *mezuzot*, doorposts. That night, gathered inside, they ate this Pesah lamb just as God had ordered Moses to tell them, "with matzah and maror (bitter herbs) shall you eat it." Matzah is the food of the Seder celebration. Its taste connects every Seder to our Seder, every telling of the Exodus to our telling.

Matzah is slave food. Near the beginning of the Seder, we hold up a piece of Matzah. In the first real introduction of the story, we say about it, "This is the bread of the poor which our families ate in the land of Egypt." Matzah therefore offers the taste of oppression and suffering; locked into its bumps and perforations is the sweat, pain, fatigue, and profound agony of those years. That is why the eating of Matzah automatically conjures our empathy. As soon as we pick it up and define it as slave food, the immediate response becomes, "All who are hungry are invited to come and eat with us. All who are in need are invited to come and celebrate Pesaḥ." Eating Matzah is remembering slavery. Remembering slavery is making sure that no one else will ever have to suffer as we have. This is the primal Jewish response. The flavor of Matzah is also the flavor of concern.

Matzah is also the food of discovery. As any Jewish child (or any former Jewish child) can tell you, you can make money (or a reasonable facsimile) by finding the missing matzah, the afikomen. Matzah is the food of hide-and-go-seek. It teaches that we can discover, with effort, that which is hidden: God, light, knowledge, purpose, the forces of good. It tells us that there is a reason to seek. The taste of matzah brings with it a sense of finding.

On Pesaḥ we are instructed by the opportunity of matzah. It is a mitzvah to eat it and assimilate that which it has to teach: the taste of the Exodus, the trace of Passovers which have gone before, the nourishment of remembered slavery with its empathic response, and the flavor of discovery—not an unbalanced diet. At the Seder, it is a specific mitzvah to eat and use matzah as an element of the retelling of the Exodus; throughout the week, the eating of matzah becomes a chance to tell and retell many important family stories.

The Elimination of Hametz: ḥametz is anti-matzah. It is any food which is made from grain or a grain product which has risen, fermented, or which potentially might have done so. The Jewish tradition has a mania about ḥametz on Pesaḥ: you can't eat it (*Deuteronomy* 16.3, *Exodus* 13.3), own it (*Exodus* 13.7), or even gain benefit from it (*Exodus* 12.9).

Tradition asks Jews to do an extensive cleaning of their dwelling places prior to Pesaḥ. This is then followed by a four-part ritual "search and destroy" process which eliminates the possibility of any ḥametz remaining.

*Mekhirat Ḥametz.* While Jews are ideally supposed to use up, give away, or destroy all ḥametz prior to Pesaḥ, in practical terms this doesn't always work. Thus, rabbinic tradition evolved a legal fiction, the selling of ḥametz. Traditionally, Jews seal the ḥametz they don't dispose of in a drawer, cabinet or closet and then enter into a contractual agreement with a non-Jew who buys that space and what is contained in it for the duration of the holiday. The sale itself has its own ritualized formula and ceremony and is one important step in the transition from normal reality to Pesaḥ's reality. Usually, individuals don't actualize their own sales, but conduct them through their synagogues or rabbis.

*Bedikat Hametz.* Cherie Koller-Fox describesBedikat Hametz as the Jewish Easter egg hunt. In the dark of the night before Pesaḥ, Jews search their houses for any remaining ḥametz. This is a ritual search, the house being already cleaned and ready. Armed with a candle for light, a wooden spoon to lift the ḥametz, and a feather to sweep it into the spoon, children search the house—hunting for the ten pieces of ḥametz which have been hidden. The search is a game, a game which ends the long period of preparation. A *brakhah* is said before it begins, a *brakhah* which reveals its true purpose: "Praised are You, Lord our God, Ruler of the universe, who has made us holy through the mitzvot, and made it a mitzvah for us to remove all h.ametz."

*Bittul Hametz.* Once the search is completed, the family goes through the third step, the recitation of a legal formula. In Aramaic, they say, "All ḥametz in my possession which I have not seen or removed—anything which I don't know about—is now nullified and ownerless; it is just like the dust of the earth."

*Bi-ur Ḥametz.* The next morning, no later than five hours after sunrise, the ḥametz found during the *bedikat ḥametz* search is burned. Again this is a ritual process. A formula similar to the one said during *bittul ḥametz* is recited. Some families also add a meditation which reveals another part of the true meaning of the war on ḥametz, "Lord, our God, and God of our ancestors, just as I have removed all ḥametz from my home and my ownership, so may it be Your will that I merit the removal of evil urges from my heart."

To understand these rituals and the tradition's obsession with the removal of ḥametz, with the creation of *Pesaḥdik*, it is important to understand the lesson of uncompromising obsession. Done right, there is no halfway Pesaḥ possible. Getting ready for the holiday has to be done "all the way." The four steps of the ḥametz removal ritual make that very clear: clean, then sell, hunt, annul and burn. In the end, no ḥametz is left—the job is complete.

Symbolically, matzah is as simple as anything ever gets; there is nothing extra or bloated. Matzah is basic. It is like our true selves—the real essence of who we should be. It can be compared with the real stuff in life: truth, love, meaning—the kinds of things which should give our lives direction. Pesaḥ begins when we get back to the level of matzah. Doing so is a process which says that freedom is not a halfway measure. It takes total dedication. While Passover preparation is a pain—much work and effort—it is also an

engaging process. Really cleaning the house is always a renewing experience. It puts you in touch with old memories, it lets you rid yourself of that which is no longer necessary, and it provides a new beginning. The physical actions all mirror spiritual achievements. Besides, done as a family, as a ritual, cleaning can be fun. Too, in our instant society, there is an important lesson in an act of careful preparation. Consider the fun of going into your child's room and seriously engaging in the discussion of "which of these toys are 'matzah' and which are 'hametz.'" In our age of public dispassion, it is nice to make a total commitment.

The Telling of the Exodus Story: Stories are the lifeblood of any culture. Seder night is the ultimate storytelling experience. It is an evening filled with experiences. Everyone has her own Seder stories. Asking the four questions, eating the horseradish, drinking four cups of wine, finding (or not finding) the afikomen, opening the door for Elijah are themes on which most Jews have a story to tell. They are those kinds of experiences. The night of telling stories is also a night on which stories are made. The night of recalling memories is also a time of making memories. That is the nature of Passover, and that especially is the nature of the Seder, the most carefully crafted and expressive of all Jewish rituals.

Running or participating in a Seder is the prime responsibility of every Jewish parent. It is the one responsibility the Torah carefully clarifies, repeating four times the mitzvah of telling the Passover story to your children. Seder running is a complex process. It involves the mastery of a complex series of rituals, of a lot of text, of the human dynamics of a crew of people around a table for several hours. It isn't easy, and it isn't always done well. It can degenerate into a lot of reading or mumbling leading up to the question, "When do we eat?" Or, it can soar, becoming a time of dynamic communication, family unity and profound learning. In the few short paragraphs we have available here, we can't begin to unpack or explain the dynamics of the Seder or provide guidance in staging one. We have created the **Building Jewish Life Haggadah** as one good tool for enabling family Seders which really work for kids. We have also had the pleasure of working with Dr. Ron Wolfson on the creation of the Federation of Jewish Men's Clubs' book, *The Art of Jewish Living: The Passover Seder*. The latter is a complete guide to both the technical and the artistic aspects of Seder leading. Either of these can be found in your local Jewish bookstore, or by calling 1-800-BE-TORAH.

As a Jewish parent, involved in providing your child with a Jewish education, your prime responsibility is that of creating a Passover experience and using it to tell—parent to child—the story of how God took us out of Egypt. This is not only your obligation—it is also your reward.

# FOOTNOTES

1. **Matzah** is the unleavened bread which is eaten on Pesah. It is made of flour and water which has been baked within 18 minutes of being mixed. While matzah can be eaten all year round, special care is given to the matzah prepared for Pesah (and labeled *Kosher L'Pesah*) making sure that it has come in contact with no hametz. Very traditional Jews use a even more carefully guarded matzah, called *Sh'murah Matzah* which has been watched from the time the wheat was harvested to prevent any possibility of fermentation (even from random moisture). For more on matzah, see the essay above.

2. **Pesah** is the Hebrew term for Passover, reflecting the fact that the angel of death *pasah* (passed over) the homes of the Jews when death came to the firstborn of all the Egyptians. Pesah also refers to the lamb which was sacrificed and eaten on the first night of Pesah. This Pesah offering was the center of the Seder experience until the Temple was destroyed and the festival was reworked into a home celebration.

3. **Mitzvah.** As we have mentioned earlier in the parents' introduction, *mitzvah* a central word in this series. It is also an ideological word, its explanation often defining the boundaries between the various branches of Judaism. Where your understanding of mitzvah is exact, use and teach that understanding. In situations where your own ideology of Jewish practice is evolving, introduce *mitzvot* as "Jewish things to do," or as "something which Jews do." Repeated context and examples will clarify its meaning more fully, and allow children to relate to many different *mitzvah*-concepts.

4. **Hametz** is the technical term for food which is not appropriate for Jewish use on Pesah. It comes from a Hebrew root which means "fermented" and categorizes anything which is made from grain which has risen or has been acted upon by yeast bacteria. For a fuller explanation, see the essay above.

5. **Haggadah** is the name of the book used to conduct the Passover table ritual. It comes from a Hebrew root which means "telling," and is designed as the vehicle for parents to use while telling the story of the Exodus through the Seder ritual. While the core of Haggadah was created by the rabbis of the Mishnah and its basic text was locked in during the fifth century, today there are more than 3,000 different Haggadot in print.

6. **Seder** means "order" in Hebrew and is the name of the ritual meal and storytelling which is held on the first and second first nights of Passover. The Seder, which has been divided into fifteen steps, incorporates the formal elements of a Jewish ritual meal: candles, *kiddush*, hand-washing, *motzi*, and *birkat ha-mazon* (Grace After Eating)—with the telling of the Exodus story via symbols, games, foods, and rituals. Seder is a talk-feast which allows us to recreate and evolve the experience of the first Passover in our own homes.

# FOR THE TEACHER

This Passover volume of the **Building Jewish Life** library centers on four objectives:

1. Students will be able to identify and explain the basic objects used in the preparation for Pesah and at the Seder: matzah—feather, spoon and candle—z'roah—maror—haroset—karpas—haggadah.

2. Students will become familiar with and achieve a level of mastery of some parts of the Seder text: Ha-lahma anya (in English), the four questions, and the individual *brakhot* over the key ritual foods.

3. Students will become familiar with the basic process of a Pesah Seder.

4. Students will become familiar with the story of the Exodus through telling it in their own way.

# ESSENTIAL VOCABULARY:

| | |
|---|---|
| 1. Matzah | Unleavened Passover Bread |
| 2. Hametz | Food made from grain which has risen |
| 3. Pesah | The Hebrew name of Passover teaching us that God "Passed Over" the Jewish homes |
| 4. Haggadah | The name of the book which helps us tell the story. |
| 5. Seder | Meaning "order" which is the service we hold at the table on the first night(s) of Pesah |
| 6. Maror | The bitter herb which reminds us of bitter slavery |
| 7. Haroset | Seder food which reminds us of the mortar used with the bricks we made when we were slaves |
| 8. Afikomen | The hidden matzah which is found for a prize. |

# ADDITIONAL VOCABULARY:

| | |
|---|---|
| Pharaoh | |
| Plague | |
| Freedom | |
| Midwife | |
| Appetizer | |
| Dayyenu | "It would have been enough." |
| Jerusalem | |

*We will assume that this material will cover four classroom sessions. Teachers should feel free to adapt and improvise according to (1) time available, (2) age and ability of students, (3) involvement of families, (4) previous background, and (5) moments of inspiration.*

# LESSON ONE:
## The Story of the Foods

1. **SET INDUCTION:** HOLD UP a piece of matzah. ASK students to identify it. ASK: "How can this piece of matzah teach us a story?" ESTABLISH that eating a piece of matzah helps us to remember an important story, the story of how we left Egypt. EXPLAIN that today we are going to learn the stories of four important Seder foods: matzah, maror, haroset, and karpas (parsley and salt water).

2. **TASTING AND TELLING:** Either through the use of four centers or all together as a class, work through these four symbolic foods. In each case use this sequence: (1) IDENTIFY the food. (2) TASTE the food. (3) TALK about the taste. (4) RECALL the story.

*Matzah* tastes simple. It reminds that our ancestors had to leave Egypt in a hurry and didn't have time for the bread to rise. When we bake matzah today, we have to hurry just as they did.

*Maror* tastes bitter. It reminds us that slavery was bitter. It was hard to live that way, just as the maror is hard to eat.

*Haroset* is sweet. The lesson comes from the looks, not the taste. Haroset reminds us of the mortar used to cement bricks together. When we were slaves the Egyptians made us make bricks and build cities for them.

*Karpas.* The salt water tastes like tears (and like the Reed Sea). It also reminds us how we cried when we were slaves.

3. **MAKING PESAH FOODS:** Using parents or student assistants, do as much of the following as possible.

　A. BAKE MATZAH: MIX flour and water, knead into dough, roll flat (using a dowel as a rolling pin), poke holes with a fork, and bake in the hottest possible oven. TIME the process. MAKE everyone finish within 18 minutes from the time you started. MAKE it a ritual. Have everyone SHOUT, *"L'shem mitzvat matzah"*—"I am making this for the mitzvah of matzah."

　B. MAKE HAROSET: Follow the recipes on page 38 in this book. If possible, make at least two different kinds.

　C. GRIND YOUR OWN HRAIN (Horseradish) Use hand graters. It is good if the kids cry. Mix the grindings with a little vinegar. Seal in a jar. Keep the air out.

4. **PASS OUT THE BOOKS:** PASS out the books. INVITE kids to page through them. Have every student PICK out and SHARE his/her favorite page.

5. **HOMEWORK:** Ask students to read the pages where the kids tell their own stories about Egypt with their parents. (page 42)

6. **CLOSURE:** HOLD UP the four foods. REVIEW the stories they tell.

# LESSON TWO
## Telling the story of the Exodus

1. **SET INDUCTION:** READ the quotation on the title page of this book. DISCUSS it. ASK: "How can we tell the story of what it was like to be a slave in Egypt?" ACCEPT all answers.

2. **MY EXODUS:** SHOW the video "My Exodus." This was made by Torah Aura Productions and has six kids telling their own stories of what it was like to go out from Egyptian slavery. The story pages in this book were taken from that video (though some of the kids have been changed because the others grew too much).

3. **TELLING STORIES:** GATHER the class in a circle. RETELL together the story of the Exodus. WORK your way through the questions below. HELP the kids to think up original answers by giving your own first.

    A. What was it like to be a slave? What job did you have?

    B. What did you hate about being a slave? Did you like anything?

    C. When Moses said that you would soon be free, what did you think?

    D. What was it like during the plagues? Look at the list on page 25. Discuss each plague.

    E. When you left Egypt, what did you take with you?

    G. What was the best part about being free?

4. **CREATIVE PROJECT:** Have students draw and/or write down one part of their own story.

5. **HOMEWORK:** ASK students to complete the exercise on page 42 with their parents.

6. **CLOSURE:** ASK: "How do we know what it was like to be a slave in Egypt?" ACCEPT all answers.

# LESSON THREE
## The Seder Order

1. **SET INDUCTION:** TEACH and DRILL the chant "*Kadesh, Urḥatz...*" It would be good to have a big chart of the steps to use both here, and when you go through the Seder. Otherwise, you can use page 15.

2. **SECOND INDUCTION:** BEFORE class, hide ten pieces of hametz wrapped in tin foil around the room. HAVE STUDENTS search for the 10 pieces. INTRODUCE *Bedikat Hametz* by reading page 8.

3. **SEDER ORDER:** GATHER the class around a desk or table. On it should be all the items needed for a Seder.

(But don't do wine glasses for the whole class—this is just a drill.) START on page 16 and read your way through the fifteen steps in the Seder. Stop to DRILL each of the blessings, the four questions, etc. After each step, REPEAT the chant from the beginning up to the step which you have just completed. HOLD UP the right objects for each step along the way.

4. **REINFORCEMENT:** WORKING in pairs, have students

COMPLETE the chart on pages 40 and 41.

5. **CLOSURE:** SING *Kadesh, Urḥatz* again. PANTOMIME all the actions.

# LESSON FOUR
## A Family Model Seder

Use this last session to hold a family-based model Seder. Be creative. You may want to do it in a home, have a wilderness Seder, etc. Let your students parents help. Have families prepare different parts of the Seder ritual and present them to the group. Have a good time. Let your families create an event which is meaningful to them. Invest your work in the organization, not in making a presentation. Let them do the presenting.